Moseley
Kings He

on old picture postcards

John Marks

MOSELEY VILLAGE, 1870.　　　　　　　PUBLISHED AT LOUIS REPOSITORY, MOSELEY.

1. A photo of Moseley Village in 1870, reproduced on a postcard mailed in March 1905 to Huntingdon. *"Am sending you a view of Moseley thirty years ago. Will do to go in your album if you have room for it"*, wrote A. Bodger to his sister. The 'Fighting Cocks' is on the extreme left, the 'Bulls Head' the white building behind the horse and trap. Published at Louis Repository, Moseley.

£3.50

Designed and Published by
Reflections of a Bygone Age
Keyworth, Nottingham 1991

Reprinted 1995, 1997, 1998, and 2000

Printed by
Adlard Print and Reprographics Limited
Ruddington, Notts

ISBN 0 946245 44 4

Front cover: High Street, Kings Heath , with Cooper's fish, fruit and poultry shop on the immediate right.

Back cover: (top): Mill Pool Hill was the rural limit of Kings Heath . The owners of car O-6050 appear to be heading away from Kings Heath to enjoy a day in the country. Postcard by Adams & Co. (no.255A), posted at Moseley in August 1915.
(bottom): The Village, Moseley.

2. The boundary between Moseley and Balsall Heath was Brighton and Edgbaston Roads. The Post Office building still stands, but the houses on the right have gone. Valentine's series postcard, published from Dundee, and postally used in January 1904.

Moseley   Institute

3. The Moseley and Balsall Heath Institute was founded in 1876 and had the building featured here built in 1883. It's now used as a dance studio, the premises having outlived the Kings Heath and Moseley Institute, built in 1878 and now demolished *(see illus. 42)*. No indication of the publisher of this card.

Moseley was constituted a separate ecclesiastical parish in 1853 from Kings Norton and Yardley, while Kings Heath was constituted in 1863 from Kings Norton. Both were then in Worcestershire, but were incorporated in the city of Birmingham in 1911.

In 1900, Kelly's Directory described Moseley as a *"pleasant suburb possessing fine scenery and containing some beautiful country houses."* As with most of the places that are now suburbs of Birmingham, Moseley and Kings Heath had changed little over the centuries before 1900, but afterwards developed out of all recognition. Such development, and population growth, were dependant on improvements in transport. Canals like the Worcester-Birmingham to the West, the Stratford-on-Avon to the South, and the Warwick-Birmingham to the North-East were too far away to benefit the area; and the Birmingham and Gloucester Railway initially had little impact, since it ran direct from Camp Hill to Kings Heath. With the opening of intermediate stations, though, the line became a viable proposition for commuter traffic. The major factor in the transport revolution, though, was undoubtedly the introduction of the trams. Frequent and rapid services enabled large numbers of people to be moved quickly, and housing development was stimulated. Large estates were sold off to provide building plots. The country lanes disappeared under terraces of houses and the fine scenic vistas of 1900 were gone for ever. This book is not intended to be a history of the area, but a nostalgic look at the villages as they changed into suburbs.

Picture Postcards were first published in Britain in 1894, but it was not until a decade later that they began to take off, when in 1902 the Post Office allowed a message to be written on the address side. This meant that the whole of one side was available for the picture and obviously gave more scope to publishers. Photographic viewcards became very popular, and the postcard became the most important way of communicating news or messages, in much the same way as the telephone is used today. The years up to 1914 were the 'Golden Age' of picture postcards, when millions of imaginative designs covering every subject under the sun were published by a host of national and local firms. There's hardly a village or hamlet that wasn't documented at that time by a postcard publisher, though sometimes the number of cards available was unrelated to the size of a community.

Birmingham had many fine publishers of postcards, and they recorded street scenes, trams, railway stations, markets and events. Some, notably George Wells Riley, Thomas Lewis and Edwards & Co. are represented in this book, along with national publishers who achieved an amazing coverage of even quite small places. Wherever the name of the publisher is known, this is included in the caption, but often postcards were published anonymously. The majority of those featured are of pre-1918 vintage; sometimes part of the message is quoted where it is relevant or interesting, and the date of postal usage — if any — is also mentioned.

John Marks, July 1991

NB. We have included this book in our 'Yesterday's Warwickshire' series, even though both Moseley and Kings Heath were in Worcestershire until 1911, during the period when many of the featured cards were published. We feel most people will associate themselves with Birmingham and Warwickshire rather than the pre-1911 county.

Kings Heath is spelt throughout without its apostrophe, though some of the captions on the actual postcards use it.

Brian Lund, Reflections of a Bygone Age.

4. Alcester Road looking down into Moseley, with the 18th century dovecote in the grounds of Moseley Hall Hospital on the left.

5. This view of Moseley was taken in the 1890s, though not published as a card until 1904. The steam tram lines run through to Kings Heath, but no redevelopment has yet taken place along Alcester Road. *(compare the next illus.)*

6. Some ten years later (c.1909) the trams have been electrified, the 'Fighting Cocks' has been rebuilt with clock tower, and new shops built on the other corner of King Edward Road. In the distance is the 'Prince of Wales' Hotel, with white lettering on the gable wall.

MOSELEY VILLAGE

7. The Bullock family of builders were long established in 19th century Moseley. Their premises were situated more or less at the point where Salisbury Road joins Alcester Road. Salisbury Road was cut through Moseley Hall Park between 1895 and 1900.

8. "The Village" was the name given to what is now St. Mary Row. The poster on the right gives details of John Morgan, advertised to speak at a public meeting. Thos. Shipton, cabinet maker, was at no. 7, while at no. 17 was Mathias Watts & Co., who only recently left the premises. Photographic card, posted in May 1907.

New year Greetings 1906.

9. The top end of "The Village", with F.S. Brecknell, watchmaker, at the single-storey building on the left which is still in use for watch repairs. The postcard, published by John Walker & Co. of London, was actually sent to Canada in December 1905.

10. Harry Wright, late manager for F. Horton & Son, painter and decorator, was at no. 54 on the left. Card by Thos. Lewis of Stratford Road, Birmingham.

11. Park Garage on Alcester Road, in the 1930s when the business was established. Part of the advertising states that there was garaging for 100 cars. The premises are now occupied by W.H. Smith.

12. Belle Walk in the grip of a very heavy frost about 1910, pictured on a card by unidentified publisher.

13. The pool and park were originally part of the grounds of Moseley Hall. When Salisbury Road was cut *(see illus. 5),* local residents, fearing the area would be built on, formed a private company to preserve it. Card published by G.E. Lewis, Dudley Street, Birmingham.

14. Picture postcards were sent to many Moseley residents notifying them of the Grand Fete in 1905. The photographer of the picture on the other side, A. Lane, had premises at 103 Victoria Parade, Alcester Road.

15. When the major inter-city routes were planned, what are now large suburbs were tiny villages not worthy of railway stations. The Birmingham and Gloucester Railway (absorbed later by the Midland and then by the L.M.S.) was built in 1840 with stations at Kings Heath and Kings Norton. Moseley was the first to be added in 1867; Northfield followed in 1869, Brighton Road in 1875, and Hazelwell in 1903 *(see illus. 37)*. This 1908 view of Moseley was published by Edwards & Co. of New Street, Birmingham, no. 144 in their "Clarence" series.

16. Photographic postcard published by Thos. Lewis with a view from the road bridge. It was postally used from Moseley in May 1907.

17. Wake Green Road, with the chimney of Sarehole Mill in the far distance in line with the road. Card published by Thos. Lewis.

18. Another Lewis card. Wake Green was originally open land that was gradually encroached upon and finally enclosed in the 18th century. Wake Green Home stood between Billesley Lane and St. Agnes Road.

S 8862 PARISH CHURCH MOSELEY

19. St. George's flag was being flown at half mast when this photograph was taken of St. Mary's Church. Published by W.H. Smith in their "Kingsway" series (S 6862), used as a Christmas card, and posted in December 1911.

20. St. Mary's Church has a history of additions and alterations. Probably originating in the 15th century, most of the building dates from around 1780. It was altered in 1823-4, added to in 1886 and 1897, altered again in 1910 and finally in 1940, when there was rebuilding after damage.

21. St. Anne's in Park Hill was designed by F. Preedy and built in 1874. This card was published by W.H. Smith.

22. St. Agnes Church in St. Agnes Road was designed by William Davis and built in 1883-4, though the tower was not completed until 1932. This real photographic card was posted from Birmingham in February 1905.

S 6858   CONVALESCENT HOME MOSELEY.

23. Moseley Hall replaced a house destroyed by rioters in 1791. At the end of the nineteenth century it was the house of Richard Cadbury, who gave it to Birmingham as a convalescent home for children in 1891. W.H. Smith 'Kingsway' series card no. S 6858, postally used in September 1910.

741   WOODROUGHS SCHOOL,
                              MOSELEY, BIRMINGHAM

24. The Woodroughs School for boys was at 36 School Road, but was demolished to make way for Moseley Church of England Primary School. The postcard, published by Hudson Studios Ltd. of Birmingham, is of 1927 vintage.

541   MOSELEY SECONDARY SCHOOL,   HUDSON STUDIOS LTD. B'HAM
                              BIRMINGHAM

25. Spring Hill Congregational College was first opened in 1830, but moved to Oxford in 1885 to become Mansfield College. For a time, the buildings and grounds were used as botanical gardens, then reverted to educational purposes as a secondary school. Another Hudson Studios postcard.

Billesley Lane Moseley.

26. Billesley Lane retained its rural aspect until the tages above were demolished in 1924. This scene *ingham Homestead Series no. 1"*; the card was

Photo. Sam. G. Mason.

0s, when many of the existing houses were built — the cot-
ographed by Sam Mason and published as *"Greater Birm-*
om Moseley to Kings Heath in May 1922.

George Wells Riley was a bookseller at 364 Ladypool Road between 1900 and 1930. He published a series of fine photographic views of roads between Moseley and Balsall Heath. There are two postcard series, one with *"Riley's Real Photo series"* bottom left (as no. 27), the other with the name of the road inserted in italic script on the left (as nos. 28-30).

27. Church Road, Moseley, with a fair crowd assembled by Mr. Riley for his camera.

28. Woodstock Road, Moseley.

29. Belle Walk, Moseley.

30. Forest Road, Moseley. This card was posted to Reading in June 1908, with the message *"Many thanks for your P.P.C. It was a very pretty view."*

31. The junction of Yardley Wood Road and Showell Green Lane on a 1910 card sent to Northfield. *"Yes, I can. I will call round tomorrow night",* wrote the sender, showing great and well-founded confidence in the postal system.

CHANTRY ROAD. MOSELEY

32. Chantry Road was built between 1890 and 1900, and this postcard view dates from some years later, being mailed from Moseley in June 1917.

33. Cotton Lane, Moseley.

34. Church Road, Moseley, on a postcard in the 'Bland' series. Miss Edith Bland was the owner of the "Fancy Repository" at 400 Ladypool Road in 1908.

35. Richard Cadbury, having given Moseley Hall *(see illus. 23)* to Birmingham, moved to Uffculme. In its turn this home was given to the city, in 1916. Fifteen years later, it became an annexe to All Saints Hospital, and later a centre for the treatment of neurosis.

36. The rear of Highbury Hall, photographed by Thomas Lewis. Note part of the extensive orchid greenhouses on the right. The Hall was designed by J.H. Chamberlain and built for Joseph Chamberlain in 1879-80. Highbury was named after the area of London where he lived as a child. When Joseph died in 1914, the house became a hospital; it was presented to the city in 1932.

37. Kings Heath was one of the original stations built on the Birmingham and Gloucester railway, opening in 1840. Card produced by Valentine of Dundee for a local firm, posted from Birmingham in October 1909.

38. The Carnegie Library at Kings Heath. Andrew Carnegie was a Scottish American philanthropist who, amongst other things, provided funds for the foundation of libraries. This one was built in the first decade of the century. Valentine's series postcard.

39. High Street, Kings Heath, with one of the electric trams, which came into service to here in January 1907, replacing the old steam trams *(see illus. 41).*

46242　　　　　　　　HIGH STREET, KING'S HEATH　　　　　VALENTINES SERIES

40. The start of High Street, looking towards Moseley. Though the shops on the right are little changed (architecturally), the area on the left in the distance – featuring a signboard "J. Ellis & Son, Coal Merchants" on this postcard – has recently been developed. Valentine's XL series card no. 46242, postally used in August 1910.

KING'S HEATH VILLAGE.

41. Steam trams first operated along Moseley Road in 1884; the line was extended to Moseley in 1886 and to Kings Heath in 1887. A depot was built in Silver Street, centre left on this card of High Street published by McCaw, Stevenson & Orr, and posted from Moseley with the message *"A bright and happy Xmas. Grannie"* in December 1903.

Kings Beath Institute & Village

42. Kings Heath and Moseley Institute was built in 1878 with money given by J.H. Nettlefold, and eventually demolished to make way for a Woolworths store. Kings Heath Board Schools, also built in 1878 on the other side of Institute Road, were only recently demolished in favour of a new row of shops. Anonymously-published card, posted from Selly Oak in June 1905.

43. A view similar to illus. 41, but taken some ten years later. Tram no. 96 is running from Hill Street on what was to become route no. 40. *"Having a good time here. The weather is simply rotten ... I went to the Grand last night ..."* wrote Gwennie to Harry in August 1915.

44. The junction of All Saints Road and Vicarage Road, with horse-drawn cab and cab stand. *"I have nearly walked these boots off my feet ... it is very open and country all round"*, ran the message on the card, posted in September 1912.

45. 'Adco' series postcard no. 329A, published by Adams & Co. of Bristol Street, Birmingham, and posted in February 1918. It shows Alcester Road with tram no. 112 on the return journey to Hill Street.

46. Cambridge Road, Kings Heath, about 1910.

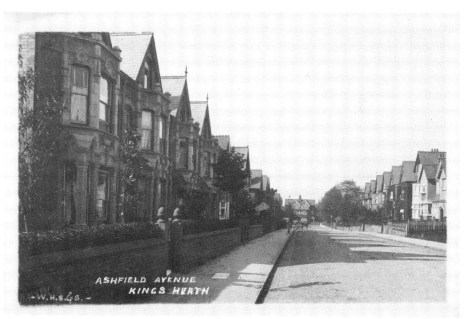

47. Ashfield Avenue, Kings Heath, on a card by W.H. Smith around the same period.

VICARAGE ROAD. KINGS HEATH.   333 A

48. Vicarage Road, with Abbots Road on the right. Another 'Adco' card, posted in August 1918.

49. Addison Road, with Goldsmith Road on the right. Thomas Onions was the grocer at Pretoria Stores, posing outside on this card with two of his female staff. The United Methodist Church adjoins the stores. Postcard used in July 1913.

50. Valentine Road, Kings Heath, in 1921, with a trio of cyclists three abreast down a deserted street.

51. Pine Apple Road, Kings Heath, about 1920.

52. Pine Apple Bridge in 1909. William Bushell's farm stands approximately where Allens Croft Road now joins Vicarage Road. Message on the card reads *"It gave me great pleasure to receive the interesting P.C. of the W. Hospital, now demolished. I have just been up into Stirchley to get this view which I hope is a new one to your collection of the Kings Heath district."*

53. Taylor Road, Alcester Lane End, on a photographic card published by Edwards & Co., and postally used in August 1913.

54. Brandwood Road in 1909.

55. Another view of the country lane on a card posted in July 1912 from "Oak Dale", Woodthorpe Road – a house situated roughly where Sunderton Road is today. *"Yesterday we went over Cadbury's Works at Bournville and had heaps of chocolates."*

56. Postcard of Mill Pool Hill on Alcester Road in the 'Crook' series, with Walker's general stores on the right. Sent from Bromsgrove in July 1920.

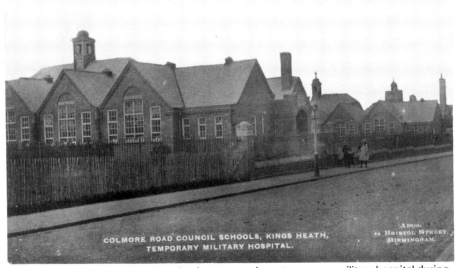

57. Colmore Road, where the schools were used as a temporary military hospital during the First World War. Harold wrote to his grandma in January 1916 on this 'Adco' postcard: *"Am sending you a view of the Hospital as promised. Have been in bed a week with influenza; quite well again now."*